# Where East Meets West

## Poems by Emma Haseldine
@strixpoems

# Where East Meets West

"I've never been"
"I've only ever been on nights out, just remember it being clean"
From two different worlds
We managed to find each other
Instantly intrigued to know more, as were you
We allowed it to flow
But kept it all on the low
The connection was there
I had to see it through
Where it was going was never to be discussed
When you'd go back to West on the weekends
With no communication, but in you I would trust
The West was now an interest of mine, because of you
Sometimes you'd miss the train to stay with me
Oh, how I gave you credit where it was due
He's from West and she's from East
There was something between them, to say the least

## 7 Months

You were nineteen when I first met you and now, you're twenty-one
If I knew the impact, you'd have on me from the start
I'd be on the run
There are seven months between us, I am older than you
You always said I never act like it, but together we grew
We stayed together when you turned twenty
The following March, you were sleeping on my day
And left me feeling empty
"I've just woken up. I was going to message you"
I knew you were lying, you just had better things to do

## December


It was you and I until the end
For every moment we spent together, I will never forget
The cold weather needn't bother us, as together we would blend
You held me and I held you, each other's secret asset
Purple lights shining through the window of your room
The settings made me feel like we could never end
But then you would send a reminder that we were just friends

## Smoke

Your room or mine?
Was always the question
We went days without eating, but together we were fine
Smoke, sleep, sex, repeat
There was no one else we would meet
You and I, twenty-four seven
If others could have seen us, we were a match made in heaven
I loved the smell of you and smoke
It would be the first thing on our minds, as soon as we woke

# January

Two thousand and eighteen had arrived
I hadn't recognised you when you first stepped inside
You were very quiet, but I just let it slide
You kept your hood on, and wouldn't accept my hug
I asked what was wrong, and all you did was shrug
December seventeen, was the best month of my life
The amount of trust you had in me
I swear I could have been a potential wife
But in January, everything had changed
I waited patiently for you to settle with me again

# Unintentional

"We were just chillin"
Our experience downplayed by you and your words
Your actions are a different story, a different meaning
The way we kissed, it came in herds
Consistent and passionate to say the least
I patiently waited until you unleashed the beast
"That was fire"
"You're gonna make me fall in love"
Everything said and done by you was unintentional
It didn't mean anything, did it?
You were so good at being dismissive
You were a professional

# Cradle

We had just recovered from our rocky patch
During our play fight, my chain you would snatch
You felt bad and tried so hard to make me stay
I stormed out in tears and screamed "go away"
You're knocking at my door and of course I let you in
I'd never seen you care so much, and in the end, you'd always win
You cradled me in your bed, knowing how upset you had made me
"Do you forgive me? Really?"
Besotted with you, I forgave within seconds
I wanted to be with you, what do you reckon?

## Contagious

Your accent will forever be with me
It showed how much time we spent together
For me to sound like I was born in the same city
"Your accent has changed Emma, is that Birmingham?"
Having a part of you in me, made me feel so pretty
You wouldn't believe when I said people had seen a change
You'd laugh it off and say something witty
You were so contagious
Living, breathing, sounding and seeing you
To others I must have sounded outrageous

# Elizabeth

A nickname you had given me, because it suited me better
I loved your motivation to succeed, trying to be a trend-setter
You changed my name in your phone to 'Lizzy'
You'd never allow me in your room if you were busy
You gave me this nickname because you thought I was posh
Treating me like a queen did not come with the name
Whenever we argued, I was always the one to blame
That's when you'd go back to calling me 'Emma'
In your Brum accent, I'll never forget it
After everything, in my room, you would come and sit
Regardless of your reasoning, we were the perfect fit

# May

You had spent a lot of time back home in West
When you came back, I knew you had missed me
I had you begging me to lay on your chest
I told you I was seeing someone new, you replied
"I don't blame you"
You still had a smile on your face, as if you could never be erased
I had to use your laptop to fill out an application
For a new place to live
With your arm around me whilst I was typing
I knew you had so much love to give
You wouldn't let me leave your room without a kiss
I said, "if you want to kiss me, you have to come here"
I'm so glad I gave in and it's not a moment I missed
Waiting by your door, you gave me one with a different twist
That someone new was immediately eliminated
"I'll leave my door unlocked"
I walked away smiling, you really had me captivated

00: 00

From West you'd always catch the last train
If you were not in the flat, within half an hour
My heart would start to experience pain
But then I'd hear the flat door open and my heart would drop
I'd instantly run to my peephole, to make sure it was you
Excited for the "you awake?" message
As I was thinking about you non-stop
I'd leave it five minutes', and eventually reply
But then you'd leave me waiting, oh how were so sly
"Come here" Was the message I'd been waiting for all night
Together we were one
And every time you came back, it felt just right

# Advice

All the advice from peers I would ignore
Another bottle of codeine you would pour
Only a little, you would allow me to try
We both knew how selfish you were inside
For hours and hours, you would sleep
I used to worry about all the deadlines you wouldn't meet
In one ear and out the other
Over FaceTime is how I'd meet your mother
Your power of action, would change the advice given to me
That's when I knew, I could never flea

## Confusion

You cannot deny that you never used to pry
Wanting to know every detail so you could feel powerful
I had mistaken your questioning for caring
You had me open up oh so flowerful
Questioning you did not sit well; you'd fail to look me in the eye
I will never forget how many times you made me cry
The affection you had shown was not normal
For someone who just wanted friendship
Confusion is an understatement
You've left me relentless

## Delusional

I won't deny, I was deluded
You were my first love, I have concluded
Your words and actions contradicted themselves
Always leaving me confused and overwhelmed
You will eventually come across these words
It will all look crazy to you
You never believed a word I said
But I guess now you'd know it's true

## No Trim

You were beautiful to me with or without a trim
You loved feeling on my body and how I am so slim
A durag was worn by you most of the time
You'd probably read this page and say
"Emma, what are these rhymes"
Laying in your bed, I was slightly sitting up
You were tired, so your head in my arms, you would tuck
Wanting more comfort, you exposed my breast
With my nipple in your mouth, finally had you at rest
Stroking your head, I felt at home
I loved watching you in the mirror
Brushing through your expired trim with a comb

## Will Power

As soon as I gave in and contacted you
I was back to square one
Besotted to say the least, you really had me spun
You'd give in and message me too
And I never had the will power to say no
Especially with that Brum accent of yours
After a night with you, people would notice me glow
I've stopped looking for distractions
Instead I'm focusing on what's good for me
We wasted each other's time; I think you'd agree

## Your Favourite

I'd wear a particular piece of lingerie
And to me, you would say
"This one is my favourite"
You would never say specifically why
Between my breasts was a pink bow tie
Maybe it was the colour complimenting my pale skin
Every time I would undress, on your face you'd have a grin
You'd run your fingers along the lace
Lying next to you, my body you would always embrace
Wearing your favourite, got me back on your good side
You'd let everything go, even your pride
"Keep it on"
You would say, but you'd have to be careful for it not to rip
Otherwise, for a new one you would pay

# Ego

Your ego is your best friend
And it would be one of the reasons why we had to end
I had damaged it many times
Which made you bitter towards me just like limes
You're the best I've ever had, and I made sure you knew
When we lived in one place, we were stuck together like glue
Your ego and pride go hand in hand
Whatever it was we had, I know in your head it wasn't planned
That's why sometimes you would move distant
And your ego would take over, then I'd move distant too
Until you came back
And we'd behave like everything was brand new

# July 14<sup>th</sup>

I told you I was staying until the end
You changed your mind and decided to stay too
In the message, you would send
"I'm doing work right now"
All I wanted was to be close to you
You accepted my help, to get you through
Up all night because you had a report due
I took away the stress and kept you calm
We reached the deadline and the sense of relief
Had your face in your palms
"Thank you" you said
I wanted to sleep so I left and said bye
The lack of emotion in you nearly made me cry
Seven FaceTime calls were missed
We could have had one last kiss
Getting out of bed, knowing you had already left
I spent the whole of that day full of regret
But I knew it wasn't the end
I typed out the words "I love you" and was brave enough to hit send

## New

Inviting you to my new flat was never in my plans
Of course, I gave in, but you wouldn't even hold my hand
Not living with each other anymore
And time apart meant I only had memories to store
It shouldn't have continued
And I held onto something that wasn't there
The amount of times you told me you were coming and let me down
Was something I really could not bare
I really wanted a new start, but from you, I could not part

3 weeks

Is how long we have gone unspoken
Do you think about me?
I've been feeling so many things, however my logic has woken
These weeks have taught me you were no good for me
Yes, you'd be pleasing one part
Another you'd leave disappointed and broken
3 weeks it has taken me
Taken me to learn about myself again and fix my heart

# Compliments

Once you teased me and said you liked me back
This was one of the lies in which you could never keep track
When you teased me, you gave me a list of compliments
From my eyes, to my humour, to my smile
You could have filled out a word document
You meant these compliments; I could see it in your eyes
My heart rate went up, that I won't deny
At that point, you knew you had me
I wasn't going anywhere, and everyone could see

# Attempts

Since we moved away from each other
No matter how many new people I would meet
I would always have to end it because I felt like a cheat
Attempting to move on was a waste of time
No one was like you, never mind us combined
You were always in the back of my head
Laughing at the guy in front of me
Looking back at things now
I should've kept purely focused on my degree
Explaining my feelings to potentials
Was becoming longer and longer
I knew with you on my mind, I wasn't getting any stronger
The attempts were pointless, as I was still wrapped up in you
The attempts of telling you I loved you was pointless
Because you still had no clue

## Reminders

You knew what you were doing
To you I was oh so edible
Leaving bruises, making us inseparable
Reminders of you on my skin
You loved leaving your mark on me
Even had you biting on my chin
You'd tell me to keep quiet so no one could listen in
I couldn't help myself, you were so deep within
Deep within my soul and other places of course
When our time was over, you'd ask me to leave with no remorse
Reminding me what we were, but I knew I'd be back again

## Control

The control you had over my mind was frightening
Feeling your hands all over my body, always had me tightening
We pleased each other in many ways
Even when apart, you'd be on my mind for days
You'd choose your words very carefully, knowing my weaknesses
After moving away, we wouldn't see each other every day
I would study the sequences
You had me in your control
Knowing you could ring whenever you'd like
Even had me missing lectures, like we were both on strike
Control is a dangerous thing
Forever onto you, I would cling

## Bad Habits

You're the worst habit I've ever had
I won't lie, you didn't always make me feel sad
But you know how sensitive I am
And it's one of the reasons we couldn't be together
My mood would change, just like the weather
I couldn't get enough of you
Lying next to you, I soaked up every moment
Reminding myself, 'you're next to him, take it all in'
I would still choose you, even if you had a twin

# +44

I lost count the amount of times I deleted your number
Of course, I knew it off by heart
It was always the same time that you would start
Start the games, but I would never complain
I drove to you one last time
You were only eight minutes down the road, of course I didn't mind
I clicked the home button on your phone
And saw I was no longer 'Lizzy'
You were neither saved on mine
And I turned to you and said, with my head feeling dizzy
"I love how we don't have each other's number saved"
You smiled and continued smoking
When the zoot was finished
It was my thigh you'd always start stroking
Kissing was our favourite part, so passionate for a plus four-four
Never again, to myself I swore

## Excuses

I made endless excuses for you
To me, you never stayed true
I must have sounded so stupid to my peers
I can't believe that shit would have gone on for nearly two years
The excuses have ended, and it's time to move on
Of course, my feelings for you are not fully gone
Let's be honest, you never really cared about me
Better without you, I will be

# Ralph Lauren – L

My vest you had ruined, meant giving me one of your tops
You found one with no hesitation
At that point you had me on lock
A large top of yours on my small body
Meant I'd be wearing it non-stop
It smelt of you and smoke
My two favourite things at the time
The large top would not be washed for a while, not even for a dime
"You can keep it"
I wasn't your girlfriend and saying that should have been a crime
You knew I was in love with you
And you knew you didn't love me back
But yet we never split, and you had codes I could never crack
You knew I wore the large top to bed
I knew you loved the thought of this in your head
There was a day that the large top was torn
As soon as I did this, I felt re-born

# Interference

Failed once again at trying to move on
Blocking your number only made me feel so strong
But after a while you'd find your way back
No caller ID was your way to attack
Next minute, I'm lying with you in bed
And you said "hi again"
I'd hate myself for allowing it to happen
When I got the map in, it's always your address I had to tap in
A reminder in the bedroom that we were never slackin'
Interfering in my recent relationship
Shame on me and shame on you for being evil about it
We were back again, back to familiarity
With us, there was never any clarity

# Honesty

This one may be a little hard to write
I was up drinking, and decided to call you late at night
Still not remembering how we got onto the topic
But you admitted you had an encounter with someone else
My heart shattered into pieces, it was really catastrophic
I was crying down the phone to you
I remember you saying my name
"Emma, don't cry"
In your stupid Brum accent, I swear I never wanted to hear it again
Ending the phone call, I threw my phone
It was devasting knowing how far apart we had grown
All I wanted was to live with you again
I knew we'd be in contact soon, but the question was when

# Connection

You know when you have a connection with someone?
Ask yourself, is it really there?
Is the energy reciprocated?
If not, then it's really just all unfair
Taking a step back, meant more room for analysis
Fooling yourself, thinking this type of relationship is rare
It's not rare, I promise you there's more out there
And when it is reciprocated
I'm sure with everyone, you will share

# Sneakin'

I know you've been lurking, your name I eventually spotted
Realising I've seen you there before, left my mind clotted
If you ever came across this page and read these lines
No doubt you'd be glad that I left you behind
You'd probably come out with your nervous feminine laugh
But then again, you always hated reading paragraphs
You don't follow me, but I saw you there
All you're getting from me now, is air

# Time

It's the best healer
Head to toe in North Face, wearing all black
You'd say I look like a drug dealer
I will forever remember the time spent with you
Even if you didn't feel the same
Publishing my poems, I'll make sure, you never forget my name
Because everything that's happened with you
Was all just a big game
I can rely on time to heal me
Your incoming No Caller ID will not be answered
I beg you just let me be

## Tipsy

There's a part of me that wants you to call
Is it the part that I should ignore?
I'm feeling to pour another fours
I bet you're thinking 'this is such a bore'
As tipsy as I am now, it's the first time I haven't fully craved you
It's definitely a feeling I'm going to have to get used to
Maybe you're just taking your time and that's fine
Or maybe you'll never react to these poems
In that case, I'll just have more wine
I'm laughing at that last line, and so should you
You know I don't take myself too seriously
One of the things you love about me
With you, I'll never get to be

# Explicit

You can't say we wasn't great at it
Always made me feel good, had you looking back at it
We loved it when the sex was more passionate than expected
None of the encounters were ever projected
It only took me lying in your bed, for you to become erected
You once called me 'evil' during sex
Continuing our then relationship, only made it more complex
How many times would you say? I've lost count
Remember all the times you wouldn't let me dismount?
I remember so many things and so many nights
All over my body you would bite
"Why is your skin so soft?"
What a stupid question
After we had finished
I was always searching for your love confession

# Different

You'd probably laugh when I say I'm not like the rest
I just want you to remember the good times we had
When we were at our best
A specific moment in time comes to mind
I doubt you'd be able to guess it
You brought out sides of me, that others cannot
Other man would hate the fact I'm not emotional enough
But they could never hit the spot
I promise you I'm not as sensitive as you think
But because I could never have you, is why my heart would sink
I know I'm writing these poems
Which may seem sensitive and emotional to you
But how else can I release the heaviness in my heart
When you and I are constantly apart

# Blocked

"Block his number" my peers would say
I always thought if I did that, I'd be betraying you in some way
It made me feel sad, but I knew I had to
In the back of my mind I knew other ways of contacting you
You knew these ways too, even if it came down to emailing me
Recently I've noticed from another account, you like to pree
You are blocked now, because I'm sick of waiting around
Sick of you watching me breakdown

## Caught

There you were again, looking on my page
I bet you think I don't see you
But of course, I do, now you can read what I went through
I'm surprised at how frequently you viewed my story
I'd never mention your name, for you to take back all the glory
I'm glad you've come across this page
Because all in all, that was my aim
I love the thought of you reading all these words
I could never say to your face
Contact is not something I expect from you
It's definitely not the case
But I know what we were like, we both loved the chase

## Finally

I finally feel a sense of relief
You wouldn't believe the way my heart used to ache over you
I hate how you thought I was always out to cause you grief
You finally know exactly how I feel
Last year when I told you I loved you, to you, it still didn't feel real
When you do, I want you to read my words carefully
Because none of it is lies
I don't expect anything from you
Because you could never sympathise

## No Exposing

You do not need to worry
I will never type out your name for others to see
There's only a couple that know, the others can just pree
Pree like I know you are now
I know you probably don't care anyhow
As long as writing makes me feel good
That's the main thing
As closure for me, it will bring

## Confidence

"She's not as confident as you"
You once said
I think that was your way of complimenting me
But I'd rather have had your love instead
It's taken time for me to build my confidence
And it's one thing you definitely haven't knocked
I remember when I changed my number
And you instantly thought you were blocked
That still makes me laugh, even till this day
My confidence is something, you could never take away

## Power

Power comes with a lot of danger
Mentally, physically, emotionally, you're able to change her
I'd never say no to you
When you were about to message or call, I always knew
Within 10 minutes, I'd be there, right beside you
No matter how rude or disrespectful, you had me hooked
You knew this, you knew you had power over me
I'd always question if you'd ever set me free

# 1 Year

This time last year you hated me
I had messed up and I was trying so hard to re-gain your trust
Because it's a must to have you around
Next month I'd tell you I have feelings for you
Rejection from you hurt more than anything
Why did you make me feel so special? For what?

The irony of telling you on Valentine's Day
As soon as you said no, I was thinking of how to take the pain away
"You know ima have to cut you off now enit?"
The Brum accent will forever haunt me, but intrigue me
My heart shattered by you, I was your benefit
Why did we become so comfortable?

You teased me and told me you liked me back
Were they lies?
I suppose I'll never know, and you'll never keep track
We continued as if I hadn't just given you
My heart, my soul, my everything
You knew, I knew, I was addicted. I couldn't bear to detach

"You're the only girl that's been here, Emma"
Music to my ears
They said you're bad for me, but I'd never listen to my peers

You know, you know
Of course, you do
You know how much, I'm in love with you

## Same City

When I told you, I was doing my third year of Uni somewhere else
Your first guess was correct, I was moving to your city
But I promise it's not because of you, so don't even try and be witty
I'll never forget the way you laughed
I still can't believe how much time has passed
You definitely knew it was coming
Then you say you're moving back home
We won't fall back into place
But if only I had a dime for every time, we did
God forbid, I put myself back into that place
We'll be in the same city, but I'll need to avoid the chase

# Expectations

People always say you shouldn't expect too much from others
Especially from those who have shown you again and again
That they do not care, not even one bit
And I knew you didn't, because you told me many times
But with you I just could not quit
I didn't want to give up on you
My expectations grew, the longer we were pursuing each other
And I wasn't in it alone, so don't deny it, don't even bother
You were hurting me, and I was hurting myself
I was too obsessed with what 'could have been'
At least I can say, my heart is clean

## Advantage

I was your advantage
Day or night, I'd be there for you
Whatever you wanted, I would do
I'd fit myself around your schedule
And I'd always allow you to pass through
Because I was your advantage, your comfort
Without you, I didn't know what to do

## Amateur

You've never had a serious relationship
I should've known you would disregard my feelings
But to me you were still so appealing
I'm still in the process of healing
So right now, I don't want any dealings
You were an amateur to my confessions
But we still continued our sessions
I swear no one could have made a better impression

# You

There were so many things I loved about you
Even when you were not being as nice
You and I all day and night
We definitely did it more than twice
You were my only friend, who I fell in love with
But to you, I wasn't even that
You were so addictive, like a drug, I needed more
Your eyes and smile, I adored
We once laid in bed kissing
In our bubble
People would've thought we went missing
It wasn't leading anywhere else
The consistency with our lips was beautiful
You were holding me so close to you
With my body against yours, it was easily latched to
I'd do anything to go back to that moment together
Moments with you, will be remembered forever

## Testing

You know when you want to ring someone
Just to see if they would answer
No doubt you would recognise the last four digits of my number
You used to test me too, messaging me a full stop
If we hadn't spoken in a while
Seeing it would have made my heart drop
But I knew you were just seeing if you blocked or not
Testing the waters, you'd ask stupid questions
You knew your way around me
Sooner or later, I'd send you a message saying
"I'll be there for three"

# Violations

These days, people are incapable of staying true
It'll be hard for someone to get to know me again
Because my feelings have been tightened up like a screw
Regardless of the violations
My heart will always stay clean
I'll always bounce back
To be the best I've ever been
And people will hate to see that
People want you to remain low
But I'm just continuing to grow

## Untouchable

There was a period where I was purely focused on you
Even though you were not mine, I was all yours
No one of the opposite sex, could touch me or talk to me
And only a few people knew
What was happening behind closed doors
When I like somebody, my eyes do not wonder
Recently, I've been so tempted to dial your number
But that's just my mind playing tricks on me
Because if you wanted to, you'd call
Just know I really loved you, above else all

## Overcoming Heartbreak

Is there even a guide to this?
Because I rah need it
The way my heart used to ache over you
I was definitely in love
Only thing that makes me feel better, is talking to the man above
You're still faintly on my mind
And you know what? That's fine
One day I'll be laughing, looking back at this
But I have a feeling you won't
If you feel the need to text or call, I beg you just don't

## Brown Eyes

Your eyes as dark as the night sky
Through your eyes, I could see into your soul
My breath shortened, I finally said goodbye
Goodbye forever, now I cannot be captured
But one look from you and I'd be re-mastered

# Ice Cold

He is as cold as ice
But he would melt a little for her
Especially at night
Until the mood turned to freezing
And he no longer needed pleasing
Back to ice cold
To her, it would never get old

# In the Night

In the night you crave his touch
Onto memories you will clutch
I promise you, in the night, it will become easier
He will slowly fade away
You'll learn to be alone
And become more content, day by day

## Unavailable

I am emotionally unavailable until further notice
My heart has been broken, and I need some time alone
Sick of these man constantly messaging my phone
No means no, I don't care for your pride
I only cared for him, but he didn't care how I felt inside
I don't believe in healing with someone there
Distance yourself, and you'll really know who cares

## The Process

Feeling empty and numb inside is a familiar feeling
But I trust in myself, and no doubt in the end, I'll be fine
Trusting the process is a part of it all
And without trust, no doubt you'll stall
This is a part of the growing experience
Embrace it, instead of drowning in it
This mindset will eventually lift your spirit

## 72 Hours

I've noticed it only takes 72 hours to feel numb again
That's how I am anyway
Writing is my way of releasing
I hope everyone finds what works for them, someday
I have no shame in writing these words
Caring about what others think, doesn't cross my mind
It hasn't done for years, and it's the way I've been re-designed
Laughing at someone venting
Shows you don't know how to release
Immaturity suits you well
72 hours, and I'm back to being at peace

## Future Me

I now know what to look out for
Thanks to you
You've made me value myself more
I now have a different view
I know you hate all this 'emotional' shit
And you're probably not reading this
But to myself, I can now recommit

## Not Everyday

It's not every day think about someone you miss
Or wish you had it different with
Because you're only holding yourself back
He used to invade my thoughts
But I soon realised there were no benefits to this cause
He's not reaching out, and he knows how I feel
Do I sit here and cry?
Or do I prepare myself for someone more real?

I

I am my biggest fan
Take that how you will
It all starts with you, and a certified plan
I've never changed or conformed to society
Something that is very rare nowadays
I've learned that most things are just a phase
I'm not doing anything that doesn't make me happy
Time is precious, and I know it's cliche
Thankful for my experiences so far, and that I've turned out this way

# Anti

Enjoying your own company too much
Can be seen as dangerous
Never been the one to 'fit in'
And I'll always be known for being courageous
Selective with who I give my energy to
Because people always refuse to see my point of view
I know I'm different from the rest
In myself, I shall reinvest

## Grateful

Sometimes we focus too much on what we don't have
It's natural of course, but we need to change
It's our thoughts we need to rearrange
Think of everything you do have and be grateful
As others may not even get a plateful
When things go wrong, it's hard to maintain positive
Try and put it into practice, it's all in the mind
If anyone has ever hurt you, I hope you stay kind

## Peak

I've reached a new level in the healing process
Yes, I still think about you
I think you could have guessed
It's taken me ages to realise that you really don't care
Over the phone, hearing your voice
Was something I couldn't bare
But I cannot show you that I am weak
We've reached our peak
Never again, will we speak

# Voicemail

I pushed my luck
And now I am blocked from ringing you
Even though I did the same
It hurts more knowing the end is true
I was intoxicated and wanted to hear your voice
Wanted you to tell me, that I am your first choice
You were laughing at all of these words
That's when I knew, you really aren't the one for me
I am done trying, it's now my time to flea

## Twenty Something

People say that males in their early twenties
Have only one thing on their mind, sex
It soon sunk in that is all you wanted from me
You are younger and less wise
Some things about you
I'm really starting to despise
But you will soon realise
What my intentions were
And that I wasn't wearing a disguise
You'll be twenty something in a few years
But I won't be around, and I won't be all ears

# Replay

You always came up in conversation
Even when talking to someone who doesn't know you
And has never met you
I'm sure it was hard to listen to
They always said that you sound horrible
And that you're evil, for what you did to me
If you had no good intentions
Why couldn't you just let me be?
Why carry on?
These questions still replay in my head
But there is no good in dwelling on you
I will have to put us to bed

## Distractions

It is becoming easier to block you out
With various distractions helping me
Life goes on, and the future is something I am excited to see
You probably have no problem with moving on
And I never cross your mind
Peace and comfort without you, I will find

# Dreams

Last night you were in my dreams
Making love, you wanted everyone to see
You still kept your t-shirt on, making sure it wasn't too intimate
It didn't stop you from being passionate and intricate
I felt every inch go in, and you'd feel me breathing heavier
You'd feel it so tight around you, you'd have to take your time
You had me in so many positions, together we were in our prime
Kissing me whilst working your hips
I didn't want it to end, and I loved the way you felt on my lips
I woke up, and realised it was just a dream
And you were probably with someone else
Doing the exact same thing, like you did to me

## Not Special

I am a special kind of girl
But not to you
You didn't see my potential
The potential I had for us
I loved your personality
Your looks were just a plus
But I am not special to you
In me you saw nothing
And apart we grew

# Naive

I have a naive soul
That I cannot control
I only see the good in people
Thinking this way can be lethal
I need to question more
Eventually things will come out
Whatever I have in store

## Urges

I have these stupid urges at the same time every night
To ring you and think 'he just might'
You might just answer and give me what I want
I want you to tell me you want me too
Tell me you love me, out of the blue
This poem wasn't meant to be about you
But I can't fight my urges
And be with someone new

## Sensitive

I'm learning more and more about myself
I've only been alive for twenty-two years
But I am so sensitive to most things
Difficulty in future relationships, it brings
I've been hurt and I feel so fragile
Take your time with me
And just be
I will eventually set myself free
Being sensitive will outgrow slowly

## Clean Hearted

Even though I have been done wrong
By many, not just you
I will stay clean hearted
And I will always stay true
I cannot continue the cycle
Of hurting someone else
That's all people seem to be doing
Bettering myself is what I'll be pursuing

## Hopeless Romantic

You know me very well
Even though you assumed a lot about me
Being a hopeless romantic
Meant I couldn't set you free
But now you have gone
And I am left with your mean words
I'll never forget our ups and downs
And how it came in herds
My first love
I learned the hard way
You never felt the same
But with my heart you would play

# Lonely

There are many nights of loneliness without you
I've been craving someone new
To fill in what is really true
I still hope you will come back one day
And you'll tell me that you're ready
That you never should have left me
In this way

# Cold

Yes, I will remain clean hearted
No, I still haven't accepted the fact that we have parted
I've started resenting a lot
Especially the way males treat me
I won't accept any meaningless words
Any contradictions or excuses
I'm done
I'm tired

## Music

It has always helped with healing
It will help get rid of this feeling
That I have inside, because of you
My healing process is something you can't take away
I still get the urge to beg you to stay
But instead I'll listen to music
Because right now, it's all that is therapeutic

# High

Why is it I always want to ring you when I'm high
Maybe it's because I am number, than when I am sober
I've learned to love the pain
I crave more of it, and that is why I ring you
But nothing from it, I will gain
I just want to be in contact with you
And feel more pain
High off your love
I'd never put anyone else above

# No Comparison

You cannot compare me to any other girl
Nobody can, as I do not even compare myself
I am strong enough to stay confident
Nobody can take that from me
Imagine if I was weak, imagine how it would be
It would be a lot deeper than it is
I'll be no comparison of his

## Maybe the End

It's the end of us
There is no trust
I can feel it
Or maybe one day you'll unblock me
Maybe I'll be the one to try you on No Caller ID
Just out of curiosity
Time will tell, if it is really the end
Thinking about you, not one more moment I will spend

Patience

I've learned to be patient with myself
The urges won't fully disappear unless I give myself time
Having patience with anything can go a long way
Everything will fall into place
I'll still leave you unblocked
Just in case

## Realisation

I've recently been told I'm part to blame for my pain
I was told many times he didn't feel the same
But still I tried my luck
And in a familiar loop, I was stuck
I essentially allowed myself to get hurt
But then I think about everything he's said and done
And think "how the fuck, did you not expect me to be sprung"
I've come to the realisation, that we're both to blame
My love life, will never be the same

## Continue

I will talk about and write about you
Until I publish all of these words
I want the world to know what we were
And more importantly, what we were not
I will continue until I find a cure
This will continue until I find peace again
Because that is what you ruined
And we wasn't even friends

## Not me

I wasn't to blame for the way you treated me
That is just the way you turned out to be
Every girl, you treat the same
The disrespect, the rudeness
But still you'll say, you're not to blame
You are lost, and it's not my fault
I've seen all sides of you
This experience, I will get through

## No Trace

There is no trace of you on my phone
No number, no pictures, no videos
Nothing of yours I own
It's freshened my perspective
Who I talk to now, is selective
Working towards forgetting you
I just hope you never ring, out of the blue

# I Remember

I remember the way you used to hold me
Late at night, you were sitting on your desk chair
Analysing my face, and even my hair
Sitting on top of you, with my bra and Adidas bottoms on
In the reflection of the window
I stared at your hands holding my waist
I loved being so close to you
My body you would always embrace

# Careful

So many people said
"Do not get involved with a boy you live with at Uni"
Did I listen? No
It happened so naturally, I couldn't help it
"Be careful, Emma"
With all the weed and all the lean
I really couldn't see what was happening around me
Sometimes I can't help but think, what we could have been

## Your Type

I will watch out for your type
Never will I ignore red flags
Or put up with someone
Just because they give good pipe
And by good pipe, I mean good dick
Your type is evil, and in my head
It's finally clicked

## Outgrowing

I can feel myself outgrowing you
And it makes me feel happy
I'm on a new journey, I have a different view
Laughing a lot more, at our encounter
How stupid I was, the thought of you is disgusting
All in all, my surroundings just needed some adjusting
Hardly on my mind
I'm getting back on my grind

# Split

I'm in two minds about you
One is still obsessed
The other couldn't care less
The second mind will definitely win
Sometimes I can still feel you on my skin
I'm split down the middle
Just like you split my heart

## Practice

I've learned your mind needs to be stronger than your emotions
Put good thoughts into practice, and watch it do justice
If you drown yourself in your emotions
There will be no room for growth
I know you've been hurt, that's you and me both
But for once, put yourself first
Because darling, most of these boys are a curse

## Psycho

Of course, a part of me still cares
Two years is a long time
The thought of not having you, I could not bare
I did something a little crazy
But I just wanted to see if you were different with others
It turns out you're not, and you showed your true colours

# The Game

I played the game you set out for me
Even though, you'd never let me win
It was always my turn to spin
Every step forward
You'd say or do something
And I'd be forced three steps backwards
Still hoping for victory
I wanted you as the prize
The cards were in your hands
And I had endless tries

.

# Loyal

I would've done anything for you
In fact, I did do anything for you
Looking back on it now, I looked very stupid
We wasn't even exclusive
I was out here trying to play cupid
What would you class us as?
Just a fuck? Nothing further
I swear I would've helped you get away with murder

## One Day

I hope one day you wake up craving me
Just like how I used to crave you
One day I want you to feel how I felt
And for you come back to me
Together we can be
One day

## Love

It is hard to establish
I definitely felt it with you, even if you didn't feel the same
I have concluded that we are both to blame
For my sorrows
Pieces of my heart you borrowed
I still need them back
In order to get back on track
My love, my forever love

# Goodbye

This is goodbye
I can no longer try
Not with you, or with anyone
Another spliff I will bun
To get rid of you
Heartbroken
But this is what it has come to